WITHDRAWN

PEKING

THE WORLD 100 YEARS AGO

Berlin

Egypt

The Cities of Japan

London

Moscow

Paris

Peking

Southern Italy

BURTON HOLMES
PEKING

FRED L. ISRAEL
General Editor

ARTHUR M. SCHLESINGER, JR.
Senior Consulting Editor

CHELSEA HOUSE PUBLISHERS
Philadelphia

CHELSEA HOUSE PUBLISHERS

EDITOR-IN-CHIEF Stephen Reginald
MANAGING EDITOR James D. Gallagher
PRODUCTION MANAGER Pamela Loos
ART DIRECTOR Sara Davis
PICTURE EDITOR Judy Hasday
SENIOR PRODUCTION EDITOR Lisa Chippendale
ASSOCIATE ART DIRECTOR Takeshi Takahashi
COVER DESIGN Dave Loose Design

First Printing

1 3 5 7 9 8 6 4 2

Library of Congress Cataloging-in-Publication Data

Holmes, Burton, b. 1870.
Peking/ by Burton Holmes; general editor Fred L. Israel; Sr. consulting editor Arthur M. Schlesinger, jr.
   p. cm. —(The world 100 years ago)
Includes bibliographical references and index.

ISBN 0-7910-4666-4 (hc). ISBN 0-7910-4667-2 (pb).

1. Holmes, Burton, b. 1870.—Journeys—China—Peking. 2. Peking (China)—Description and travel. I. Israel, Fred L. II. Schlesinger, Arthur Meier, 1917- . III. Title. IV. Series: Holmes, Burton, b. 1870. World 100 Years Ago today.
DS795.H53   1997
915.1'1560459—dc21   97-39521
                                                          CIP

CONTENTS

THE GREAT GLOBE TROTTER

By Irving Wallace

One day in the year 1890, Miss Nellie Bly, of the *New York World,* came roaring into Brooklyn on a special train from San Francisco. In a successful effort to beat Phileas Fogg's fictional 80 days around the world, Miss Bly, traveling with two handbags and flannel underwear, had circled the globe in 72 days, 6 hours, and 11 minutes. Immortality awaited her.

Elsewhere that same year, another less-publicized globe-girdler made his start toward immortality. He was Mr. Burton Holmes, making his public debut with slides and anecdotes ("Through Europe With a Kodak") before the Chicago Camera Club. Mr. Holmes, while less spectacular than his feminine rival, was destined, for that very reason, soon to dethrone her as America's number-one traveler.

Today, Miss Bly and Mr. Holmes have one thing in common: In the mass mind they are legendary vagabonds relegated to the dim and dusty past of the Iron Horse and the paddle-wheel steamer. But if Miss Bly, who shuffled off this mortal coil in 1922, is now only a part of our folklore, there are millions to testify that

Mr. Burton Holmes, aged seventy-six, is still very much with us.

Remembering that Mr. Holmes was an active contemporary of Miss Bly's, that he was making a livelihood at traveling when William McKinley, John L. Sullivan, and Admiral Dewey ruled the United States, when Tony Pastor, Lily Langtry, and Lillian Russell ruled the amusement world, it is at once amazing and reassuring to pick up the daily newspapers of 1946 and find, sandwiched between advertisements of rash young men lecturing on "Inside Stalin" and "I Was Hitler's Dentist," calm announcements that tomorrow evening Mr. Burton Holmes has something more to say about "Beautiful Bali."

Burton Holmes, a brisk, immaculate, chunky man with gray Vandyke beard, erect bearing, precise speech ("folks are always mistaking me for Monty Woolley," he says, not unhappily), is one of the seven wonders of the entertainment world. As Everyman's tourist, Burton Holmes has crossed the Atlantic Ocean thirty times, the Pacific Ocean twenty times, and has gone completely around the world six times. He has spent fifty-five summers abroad, and recorded a half million feet of film of those summers. He was the first person to take motion picture cameras into Russia and Japan. He witnessed the regular decennial performance of the Passion Play at Oberammergau in 1890, and attended the first modern Olympics at Athens in 1896. He rode on the first Trans-Siberian train across Russia, and photographed the world's first airplane meet at Rheims.

As the fruit of these travels, Burton Holmes has delivered approximately 8,000 illustrated lectures that have grossed, according to an estimate by *Variety,* five million dollars in fifty-three winters. Because he does not like to be called a lecturer— "I'm a performer," he insists, "and I have performed on more legitimate stages than platforms"—he invented the word "travelogue" in London to describe his activity.

His travelogues, regarded as a fifth season of the year in most communities, have won him such popularity that he holds the record for playing in the longest one-man run in American show business. In the five and a half decades past, Burton Holmes has successively met the hectic competition of big-time vaudeville, stage, silent pictures, radio, and talking pictures, and he has survived them all.

At an age when most men have retired to slippered ease or are hounded by high blood pressure, Burton Holmes is more active and more popular than ever before. In the season just finished, which he started in San Francisco during September, 1945, and wound up in New York during April, 1946, Holmes appeared in 187 shows, a record number. He averaged six travelogues a week, spoke for two hours at each, and did 30 percent more box-office business than five years ago. Not once was a scheduled lecture postponed or canceled. In fact, he has missed only two in his life. In 1935, flying over the Dust Bowl, he suffered laryngitis and was forced to bypass two college dates. He has never canceled an appearance before a paid city audience. Seven years ago, when one of his elderly limbs was fractured in an automobile crack-up in Finland, there was a feeling that Burton Holmes might not make the rounds. When news of the accident was released, it was as if word had gone out that Santa Claus was about to cancel his winter schedule. But when the 1939 season dawned, Burton Holmes rolled on the stage in a wheelchair, and from his seat of pain (and for 129 consecutive appearances thereafter), he delivered his travel chat while 16-mm film shimmered on the screen beside him.

Today, there is little likelihood that anything, except utter extinction, could keep Holmes from his waiting audiences. Even now, between seasons, Holmes is in training for his next series—150 illustrated lectures before groups in seventeen states.

Before World War II, accompanied by Margaret Oliver, his wife of thirty-two years, Holmes would spend his breathing spells on summery excursions through the Far East or Europe. While aides captured scenery on celluloid, Holmes wrote accompanying lecture material in his notebooks. Months later, he would communicate his findings to his cult, at a maximum price of $1.50 per seat. With the outbreak of war, Holmes changed his pattern. He curtailed travel outside the Americas. This year, except for one journey to Las Vegas, Nevada, where he personally photographed cowboy cutups and shapely starlets at the annual Helldorado festival, Holmes has been allowing his assistants to do all his traveling for him.

Recently, one crew, under cameraman Thayer Soule, who helped shoot the Battle of Tarawa for the Marines, brought Holmes a harvest of new film from Mexico. Another crew, after four months in Brazil last year, and two in its capital this year, returned to Holmes with magnificent movies. Meantime, other crews, under assignment from Holmes, are finishing films on Death Valley, the West Indies, and the Mississippi River.

In a cottage behind his sprawling Hollywood hilltop home, Holmes is busy, day and night, sorting the incoming negative, cutting and editing it, and rewriting lectures that will accompany the footage this winter. He is too busy to plan his next trip. Moreover, he doesn't feel that he should revisit Europe yet. "I wouldn't mind seeing it," he says, "but I don't think my public would be interested. My people want a good time, they want escape, they want sweetness and light, beauty and charm. There is too much rubble and misery over there now, and I'll let those picture magazines and Fox Movietone newsreels show all that. I'll wait until it's tourist time again."

When he travels, he thinks he will visit three of the four accessible places on earth that he has not yet seen. One is Tahiti, which he barely missed a dozen times, and the other two are Iran and Iraq. The remaining country that he has not seen, and has no wish to see, is primitive Afghanistan. Of all cities on earth, he would most like to revisit Kyoto, once capital of Japan. He still recalls that the first movies ever made inside Japan were ones he made in Kyoto, in 1899. The other cities he desires to revisit are

Venice and Rome. The only island for which he has any longing is Bali—"the one quaint spot on earth where you can really get away from it all."

In preparing future subjects, Holmes carefully studies the success of his past performances. Last season, his two most popular lectures in the East were "California" and "Adventures in Mexico." The former grossed $5,100 in two Chicago shows; the latter jammed the St. Louis Civic Auditorium with thirty-five hundred potential señores and señoritas. Holmes will use these subjects again, with revisions, next season, and add some brand-new Latin American and United States topics. He will sidestep anything relating to war. He feels, for example, that anything dealing with the once exotic Pacific islands might have a questionable reception—"people will still remember those white crosses they saw in newsreels of Guadalcanal and Iwo Jima."

Every season presents its own obstacles, and the next will challenge Holmes with a new audience of travel-sated and disillusioned ex-GI's. Many of these men, and their families, now know that a South Sea island paradise means mosquitoes and malaria and not Melville's Fayaway and Loti's Rarahu. They know Europe means mud and ruins and not romance. Nevertheless, Holmes is confident that he will win these people over.

"The veterans of World War II will come to my travelogues just as their fathers did. After the First World War, I gave illustrated lectures on the sights of France, and the ex-doughboys enjoyed them immensely. But I suppose there's no use comparing that war to this. The First World War was a minor dispute between gentlemen. In this one, the atrocities and miseries will be difficult to forget. I know I can't give my Beautiful Italy lecture next season to men who know Italy only as a pigsty, but you see, in my heart Italy is forever beautiful, and I see things in Italy they can't see, poor fellows. How could they? . . . Still, memory is frail, and one day these boys will forget and come to my lectures not to hoot but to relive the better moments and enjoy themselves."

While Burton Holmes prepares his forthcoming shows, his business manager, a slightly built dynamo named Walter Everest, works on next season's bookings. Everest contacts organizations interested in sponsoring a lecture series, arranges dates and prices, and often leases auditoriums on his own. Everest concentrates on cities where Holmes is known to be popular, Standing Room Only cities like New York, Boston, Philadelphia, Chicago, Los Angeles. On the other hand, he is cautious about the cities where Holmes has been unpopular in the past—Toledo, Cleveland, Indianapolis, Cincinnati. The one city Holmes now avoids entirely is Pomona, California, where, at a scheduled Saturday matinee, he found himself facing an almost empty house. The phenomenon of a good city or a poor city is inexplicable. In rare cases, there may be a reason for failure, and then Holmes will attempt to resolve it. When San Francisco was stone-deaf to Holmes, investigation showed that he had been competing with the annual opera season. Last year, he rented a theater the week before the opera began. He appeared eight times and made a handsome profit.

Once Holmes takes to the road for his regular season, he is a perpetual-motion machine. Leaving his wife behind, he barnstorms with his manager, Everest, and a projectionist, whirling to Western dates in his Cadillac, making long hops by plane, following the heavier Eastern circuit by train. Holmes likes to amaze younger men with his activities during a typical week. If he speaks in Detroit on a Tuesday night, he will lecture in Chicago on Wednesday evening, in Milwaukee on Thursday, be back in Chicago for Friday evening and a Saturday matinee session, then go on to Kansas City on Sunday, St. Louis on Monday, and play a return engagement in Detroit on Tuesday.

This relentless merry-go-round (with Saturday nights off to attend a newsreel "and see what's happening in the world") invigorates Holmes, but grinds his colleagues to a frazzle. One morning last season, after weeks of trains and travel, Walter

Everest was awakened by a porter at six. He rose groggily, sat swaying on the edge of his berth trying to put on his shoes. He had the look of a man who had pushed through the Matto Grosso on foot. He glanced up sleepily, and there, across the aisle, was Holmes, fully dressed, looking natty and refreshed. Holmes smiled sympathetically. "I know, Walter," he said, "this life is tiring. One day both of us ought to climb on some train and get away from it all."

In his years on the road, Holmes has come to know his audience thoroughly. He is firm in the belief that it is composed mostly of traveled persons who wish to savor the glamorous sights of the world again. Through Burton, they relive their own tours. Of the others, some regard a Holmes performance as a preview. They expect to travel; they want to know the choice sights for their future three-month jaunt to Ecuador. Some few, who consider themselves travel authorities, come to a Holmes lecture to point out gleefully the good things that he missed. "It makes them happy," Holmes says cheerfully. Tomorrow's audience, for the most, will be the same as the one that heard the Master exactly a year before. Generations of audiences inherit Holmes, one from the other.

An average Holmes lecture combines the atmosphere of a revival meeting and a family get-together at which home movies are shown. A typical Holmes travelogue begins in a brightly lit auditorium, at precisely three minutes after eight-thirty. The three minutes is to allow for latecomers. Holmes, attired in formal evening clothes, strides from the wings to center stage. People applaud; some cheer. Everyone seems to know him and to know exactly what to expect. Holmes smiles broadly. He is compact, proper, handsome. His goatee dominates the scene. He has worn it every season, with the exception of one in 1895 (when, beardless, he somewhat resembled Paget's Sherlock Holmes). Now, he speaks crisply. He announces that this is the third lecture of his fifty-fourth season. He announces his subject—"Adventures in Mexico."

He walks to one side of the stage, where a microphone is standing. The lights are dimmed. The auditorium becomes dark. Beyond the fifth row, Holmes cannot be seen. The all-color 16-mm film is projected on the screen. The film opens, minus title and credits, with a shot through the windshield of an automobile speeding down the Pan-American Highway to Monterrey. Holmes himself is the sound track. His speech, with just the hint of a theatrical accent, is intimate, as if he were talking in a living room. He punctuates descriptive passages with little formal jokes. When flowers and orange trees of Mexico are on the screen, he says, "We have movies and talkies, but now we should have smellies and tasties"—and he chuckles.

The film that he verbally captions is a dazzling, uncritical montage of Things Mexican. There is a señora selling tortillas, and close-ups of how tortillas are made. There is a bullfight, but not the kill. There is snow-capped Popocatepetl, now for sale at the bargain price of fifteen million dollars. There are the pyramids outside Mexico City, older than those of Egypt, built by the ancient Toltecs who went to war with wooden swords so that they would not kill their enemies.

Holmes's movies and lectures last two hours, with one intermission. The emphasis is on description, information, and oddity. Two potential ingredients are studiously omitted. One is adventure, the other politics. Holmes is never spectacular. "I want nothing dangerous. I don't care to emulate the explorers, to risk my neck, to be the only one or the first one there. Let others tackle the Himalayas, the Amazon, the North Pole, let them break the trails for me. I'm just a Cook's tourist, a little ahead of the crowd, but not too far ahead." Some years ago, Holmes did think that he was an explorer, and became very excited about it, he now admits sheepishly. This occurred in a trackless sector of Northern Rhodesia. Holmes felt that he had discovered a site never before seen by an outsider. Grandly, he planted the flag of the Explorers

Club, carefully he set up his camera, and then, as he prepared to shoot, his glance fell upon an object several feet away—an empty Kodak carton. Quietly, he repacked and stole away—and has stayed firmly on the beaten paths ever since.

As to politics, it never taints his lectures. He insists neither he nor his audiences are interested. "When you discuss politics," he says, "you are sure to offend." Even after his third trip to Russia, he refused to discuss politics. "I am a traveler," he explained at that time, "and not a student of political and economic questions. To me, Communism is merely one of the sights I went to see."

However, friends know that Holmes has his pet panacea for the ills of the world. He is violent about the gold standard, insisting that it alone can make all the world prosperous. Occasionally, when the mood is on him, and against his better judgment, he will inject propaganda in favor of the gold standard into an otherwise timid travelogue.

When he is feeling mellow, Holmes will confess that once in the past he permitted politics to intrude upon his sterile chitchat. It was two decades ago, when he jousted with Prohibition. While not a dedicated drinking man, Holmes has been on a friendly basis with firewater since the age of sixteen. In the ensuing years, he has regularly, every dusk before dinner, mixed himself one or two highballs. Only once did he try more than two, and the results were disastrous. "Any man who drinks three will drink three hundred," he now says righteously. Holmes felt that Prohibition was an insult to civilized living. As a consequence of this belief, his audiences during the days of the Eighteenth Amendment were often startled to hear Holmes extol the virtues of open drinking, in the middle of a placid discourse on Oberammergau or Lapland. "Sometimes an indignant female would return her tickets to the rest of my series," he says, "but there were others, more intelligent, to take her place."

This independent attitude in Holmes was solely the product of his personal success. Born in January, 1870, of a financially secure, completely cosmopolitan Chicago family, he was able to be independent from his earliest days. His father, an employee in the Third National Bank, distinguished himself largely by lending George Pullman enough cash to transform his old day coaches into the first Pullman Palace Sleeping Cars, and by refusing a half interest in the business in exchange for his help. Even to this day, it makes Burton Holmes dizzy to think of the money he might have saved in charges for Pullman berths.

Holmes's interest in show business began at the age of nine when his grandmother, Ann W. Burton, took him to hear John L. Stoddard lecture on the Passion Play at Oberammergau. Young Holmes was never the same again. After brief visits to faraway Florida and California, he quit school and accompanied his grandmother on his first trip abroad. He was sixteen and wide-eyed. His grandmother, who had traveled with her wine-salesman husband to France and Egypt and down the Volga in the sixties, was the perfect guide. But this journey through Europe was eclipsed, four years later, by a more important pilgrimage with his grandmother to Germany. The first day at his hotel in Munich, Holmes saw John L. Stoddard pass through the lobby reading a Baedeker. He was petrified. It was as if he had seen his Maker. Even now, over a half century later, when Holmes speaks about Stoddard, his voice carries a tinge of awe. For eighteen years of the later nineteenth century, Stoddard, with black-and-white slides and magnificent oratory, dominated the travel-lecture field. To audiences, young and old, he was the most romantic figure in America. Later, at Oberammergau, Holmes sat next to Stoddard through the fifteen acts of the Passion Play and they became friends.

When Holmes returned to the States, some months after Nellie Bly had made her own triumphal return to Brooklyn, he showed rare Kodak negatives of his travels to fellow members of the Chicago Camera Club. The members were impressed, and one suggested that these be mounted as slides and shown to the general public. "To take the edge off the silence, to keep the show moving," says Holmes, "I wrote an account of my journey and read it, as the stereopticon man changed slides." The show, which grossed the club $350, was Holmes's initial travelogue. However, he dates the beginning of his professional career from three years later, when he appeared under his own auspices with hand-colored slides.

After the Camera Club debut, Holmes did not go immediately into the travelogue field. He was not yet ready to appreciate its possibilities. Instead, he attempted to sell real estate, and failed. Then he worked for eight dollars a week as a photo supply clerk. In 1902, aching with wanderlust, he bullied his family into staking him to a five-month tour of Japan. On the boat he was thrilled to find John L. Stoddard, also bound for Japan. They became closer friends, even though they saw Nippon through different eyes. "The older man found Japan queer, quaint, comfortless, and almost repellent," Stoddard's son wrote years later. "To the younger man it was a fairyland." Stoddard invited Holmes to continue on around the world with him, but Holmes loved Japan and decided to remain.

When Holmes returned to Chicago, the World's Columbian Exposition of 1893 was in full swing. He spent months at the Jackson Park grounds, under Edison's new electric lights, listening to Lillian Russell sing, Susan B. Anthony speak, and watching Sandow perform feats of strength. With rising excitement, he observed Jim Brady eating, Anthony Comstock snorting at Little Egypt's hootchy-kootchy, and Alexander Dowie announcing himself as the Prophet Elijah III.

In the midst of this excitement came the depression of that year. Holmes's father suffered. "He hit the wheat pit at the wrong time, and I had to go out on my own," says Holmes. "The photo supply house offered me fifteen dollars a week to return. But I didn't want to work. The trip to Japan, the Oriental exhibits of the Exposition, were still on my mind. I thought of

Stoddard. I thought of the slides I'd had hand-colored in Tokyo. That was it, and it wasn't work. So I hired a hall and became a travel lecturer."

Copying society addresses from his mother's visiting list, and additional addresses from *The Blue Book,* Holmes mailed two thousand invitations in the form of Japanese poem-cards. Recipients were invited to two illustrated lectures, at $1.50 each, on "Japan—the Country and the Cities." Both performances were sellouts. Holmes grossed $700.

For four years Holmes continued his fight to win a steady following, but with only erratic success. Then, in 1897, when he stood at the brink of defeat, two events occurred to change his life. First, John L. Stoddard retired from the travel-lecture field and threw the platforms of the nation open to a successor. Second, Holmes supplemented colored slides with a new method of illustrating his talks. As his circular announced, "There will be presented for the first time in connection with a course of travel lectures a series of pictures to which a modern miracle has added the illusion of life itself—the reproduction of recorded motion."

Armed with his jumpy movies—scenes of the Omaha fire department, a police parade in Chicago, Italians eating spaghetti, each reel running twenty-five seconds, with a four-minute wait between reels—Burton Holmes invaded the Stoddard strongholds in the East. Stoddard came to hear him and observe the newfangled movies. Like Marshal Foch who regarded the airplane as "an impractical toy," Stoddard saw no future in the motion picture. Nevertheless, he gave young Holmes a hand by insisting that Augustin Daly lease his Manhattan theater to the newcomer. This done, Stoddard retired to the Austrian Tyrol, and Holmes went on to absorb Stoddard's audiences in Boston and Philadelphia and to win new followers of his own throughout the nation.

His success assured, Holmes began to gather material with a vigor that was to make him one of history's most indefatigable travelers. In 1900, at the Paris Exposition, sitting in a restaurant built like a Russian train, drinking vodka while a colored panorama of Siberia rolled past his window, he succumbed to this unique advertising of the new Trans-Siberian railway and bought a ticket. The trip in 1901 was a nightmare. After ten days on the Trans-Siberian train, which banged along at eleven miles an hour, Holmes was dumped into a construction train for five days, and then spent twenty-seven days on steamers going down the Amur River. It took him forty-two and a half days to travel from Moscow to Vladivostok.

But during that tour, he had one great moment. He saw Count Leo Tolstoi at Yasnaya Polyana, the author's country estate near Tula. At a dinner in Moscow, Holmes met Albert J. Beveridge, the handsome senator from Indiana. Beveridge had a letter of introduction to Tolstoi and invited Holmes and his enormous 60-mm movie camera to come along. Arriving in a four-horse landau, the Americans were surprised to find Tolstoi's house dilapidated. Then, they were kept waiting two hours. At last, the seventy-three-year-old, white-bearded Tolstoi, nine years away from his lonely death in a railway depot, appeared. He was attired in a mujik costume. He invited his visitors to breakfast, then conversed in fluent English. "He had only a slight accent, and he spoke with the cadence of Sir Henry Irving," Holmes recalls.

Of the entire morning's conversation, Holmes remembers clearly only one remark. That was when Tolstoi harangued, "There should be no law. No man should have the right to judge or condemn another. Absolute freedom of the individual is the only thing that can redeem the world. Christ was a great teacher, nothing more!" As Tolstoi continued to speak, Holmes quietly set up his movie camera. Tolstoi had never seen one before. He posed stiffly, as for a daguerreotype. When he thought that it was over, and resumed his talking, Holmes began actual shooting. This priceless film never reached the screen. Senator Beveridge was then a presidential possibility. His managers feared that this film of Beveridge with a Russian radical might be used by his opponents. The film was taken from Holmes and destroyed. Later, when he was not even nominated for the presidency, Beveridge wrote an apology to Holmes, "for this destruction of so valuable a living record of the grand old Russian."

In 1934, at a cost of ten dollars a day, Holmes spent twenty-one days in modern Soviet Russia. He loved the ballet, the omelets, the Russian rule against tipping, and the lack of holdups. He went twice to see the embalmed Lenin, fascinated by the sight of "his head resting on a red pillow like that of a tired man asleep."

Although Holmes's name had already appeared on eighteen travel volumes, this last Russian trip inspired him to write his first and only original book. The earlier eighteen volumes, all heavily illustrated, were offered as a set, of which over forty thousand were sold. However, they were not "written," but were actually a collection of lectures delivered orally by Holmes. The one book that he wrote as a book, *The Traveler's Russia,* published in 1934 by G.P. Putnam's Sons, was a failure. Holmes has bought the remainders and passes them out to guests with a variety of inscriptions. In a serious mood he will inscribe, "To travel is to possess the world." In a frivolous mood, he will write "With love from Tovarich Burtonovich Holmeski."

In the five decades past, Holmes has kept himself occupied with a wide variety of pleasures, such as attending Queen Victoria's Golden Jubilee in London, chatting with Admiral Dewey in Hong Kong, driving the first automobile seen in Denmark, and photographing a mighty eruption of Vesuvius.

In 1918, wearing a war correspondent's uniform, he shot army scenes on the Western Front and his films surpassed those of the poorly organized newsreel cameramen. In 1923, flying for the first time, he had his most dangerous experience, when his plane almost crashed between Toulouse and Rabat. Later, in

Berlin, he found his dollar worth ten million marks, and in Africa he interviewed Emperor Haile Selassie in French, and, closer to home, he flew 20,000 miles over Central and South America.

Burton Holmes enjoys company on his trips. By coincidence, they are often celebrities. Holmes traveled through Austria with Maria Jeritza, through Greece with E.F. Benson, through the Philippines with Dr. Victor Heiser. He covered World War I with Harry Franck, wandered about Japan with Lafcadio Hearn's son, crossed Ethiopia with the Duke of Gloucester. He saw Hollywood with Mary Pickford, Red Square with Alma Gluck, and the Andes with John McCutcheon.

Of the hundreds of travelogues that Holmes has delivered, the most popular was "The Panama Canal." He offered this in 1912, when the "big ditch" was under construction, and news-hungry citizens flocked to hear him. Among less timely subjects, his most popular was the standard masterpiece on Oberammergau, followed closely by his illustrated lectures on the "Frivolities of Paris," the "Canals of Venice," the "Countryside of England" and, more currently, "Adventures in Mexico." Burton Holmes admits that his greatest failure was an elaborate travelogue on Siam, even though it seemed to have everything except Anna and the King thereof. Other failures included travelogues on India, Burma, Ethiopia, and—curiously—exotic Bali. The only two domestic subjects to fizzle were "Down in Dixie" in 1915 and "The Century of Progress Exposition" in 1932.

All in all, the success of Holmes's subjects has been so consistently high that he has never suffered seriously from competition. One rival died, another retired eight years ago. "I'm the lone survivor of the magic-lantern boys," says Holmes. Of the younger crowd, Holmes thought that Richard Halliburton might become his successor. "He deserved to carry the banner," says Holmes. "He was good-looking, with a fine classical background, intelligent, interesting, and he really did those darn-fool stunts." Halliburton, who had climbed the Matterhorn, swum the Hellespont, followed the Cortés train through Mexico, lectured with slides. "I told him to throw away the slides," says Holmes. "He was better without them, his speech was so colorful." When Halliburton died attempting to sail a Chinese junk across the Pacific, Holmes decided to present an illustrated lecture on "The Romantic Adventures of Richard Halliburton." He used his own movies but, in the accompanying talk, Halliburton's written text. "It was a crashing failure," sighs Holmes. "His millions of fans did not want to hear me, and my fans did not want to know about him."

For a while, Hollywood appeared to be the travelogue's greatest threat. Holmes defeated this menace by marriage with the studios. He signed a contract with Paramount, made fifty-two travel shorts each year, between 1915 and 1921. Then, with the advent of talking pictures, Holmes joined Metro-Goldwyn-Mayer and made a series of travelogues, released in English, French, Italian, Spanish. In 1933, he made his debut in radio, and in 1944 made his first appearance on television.

Today, safe in the knowledge that he is an institution, Holmes spends more and more time in his rambling, plantation-style, wooden home, called "Topside," located on a hill a mile above crowded Hollywood Boulevard. This dozen-roomed brown house, once a riding club for silent day film stars, and owned for six years by Francis X. Bushman (who gave it Hollywood's first swimming pool, where Holmes now permits neighborhood children to splash), was purchased by Holmes in 1930. "I had that M-G-M contract," he says, "and it earned me a couple of hundred thousand dollars. Well, everyone with a studio contract immediately gets himself a big car, a big house, and a small blonde. I acquired the car, the house, but kept the blonde a mental acquisition." For years, Holmes also owned a Manhattan duplex decorated with costly Japanese and Buddhist treasures, which he called "Nirvana." Before Pearl Harbor, Holmes sold the duplex, with its two-million-dollar collection of furnishings, to Robert Ripley, the cartoonist and oddity hunter.

Now, in his rare moments of leisure, Holmes likes to sit on the veranda of his Hollywood home and chat with his wife. Before he met her, he had been involved in one public romance. Gossips, everywhere, insisted that he might marry the fabulous Elsie de Wolfe, actress, millionaire decorator, friend of Oscar Wilde and Sarah Bernhardt, who later became Lady Mendl. Once, in Denver, Holmes recalls, a reporter asked him if he was engaged to Elsie de Wolfe. Holmes replied, curtly, No. That afternoon a banner headline proclaimed: BURTON HOLMES REFUSES TO MARRY ELSIE DE WOLFE!

Shortly afterward, during a photographic excursion, Holmes met Margaret Oliver who, suffering from deafness, had taken up still photography as an avocation. In 1914, following a moonlight proposal on a steamer's deck, he married Miss Oliver in New York City's St. Stephen's Episcopal Church, and took her to prosaic Atlantic City for the first few days of their honeymoon, then immediately embarked on a long trip abroad.

When his wife is out shopping, Holmes will stroll about his estate, study his fifty-four towering palm trees, return to the veranda for a highball, thumb through the *National Geographic,* play with his cats, or pick up a language textbook. He is on speaking terms with eight languages, including some of the Scandinavian, and is eager to learn more. He never reads travel books. "As Pierre Loti once remarked, 'I don't read. It might ruin my style,'" he explains.

He likes visitors, and he will startle them with allusions to his earlier contemporaries. "This lawn part reminds me of the one at which I met Emperor Meiji," he will say. Meiji, grandfather of Hirohito, opened Japan to Commodore Perry. When visitors ask for his travel advice, Holmes invariably tells them to see the Americas first. "Why go to Mont St. Michel?" he asks. "Have you seen Monticello?"

But when alone with his wife and co-workers on the veranda,

and the pressure of the new season is weeks away, he will loosen his blue dressing gown, inhale, then stare reflectively out over the sun-bathed city below.

"You know, this is the best," he will say softly, "looking down on this Los Angeles. It is heaven. I could sit here the rest of my life." Then, suddenly, he will add, "There is so much else to see and do. If only I could have another threescore years upon this planet. If only I could know the good earth better than I do."

Note: Irving Wallace (1916-1990) wrote this article on the occasion of Burton Holmes's 77th birthday. It was originally printed in *The Saturday Evening Post* May 10, 1947. Holmes retired the following year from presenting his travelogues in person. He died in 1958 at age 88. His autobiography, *The World is Mine,* was published in 1953.

Reprinted by permission of Mrs. Sylvia Wallace.

BURTON HOLMES

By Arthur M. Schlesinger, jr.

B urton Holmes!—forgotten today, but such a familiar name
in America in the first half of the 20th century, a name then
almost synonymous with dreams of foreign travel. In the era
before television brought the big world into the households of
America, it was Burton Holmes who brought the world to millions of Americans in crowded lecture halls, and did so indefati-
gably for 60 years. I still remember going with my mother in the
1920s to Symphony Hall in Boston, watching the brisk, compact
man with a Vandyke beard show his films of Venice or Bali or
Kyoto and describe foreign lands in engaging and affectionate
commentary.

Burton Holmes invented the word "travelogue" in 1904. He
embodied it for the rest of his life. He was born in Chicago in
1870 and made his first trip abroad at the age of 16. Taking a
camera along on his second trip, he mounted his black-and-
white negatives on slides and showed them to friends in the
Chicago Camera Club. "To keep the show moving," he said
later, "I wrote an account of my journey and read it, as the stere-

opticon man changed slides." He had discovered his métier. Soon he had his slides hand-colored and was in business as a professional lecturer. In time, as technology developed, slides gave way to moving pictures.

Holmes was a tireless traveler, forever ebullient and optimistic, uninterested in politics and poverty and the darker side of life, in love with beautiful scenery, historic monuments, picturesque customs, and challenging trips. He was there at the Athens Olympics in 1896, at the opening of the Trans-Siberian railway, at the Passion Play in Oberammergau. His popular lectures had such titles as "The Magic of Mexico," "The Canals of Venice," "The Glories and Frivolities of Paris." His illustrated travel books enthralled thousands of American families. He also filmed a series of travelogues—silent pictures for Paramount, talkies for Metro-Goldwyn-Mayer.

He wanted his fellow countrymen to rejoice in the wonders of the great globe. "I'm a Cook's tourist," he said, referring to the famous tours conducted by Thomas Cook and Sons, "reporting how pleasant it is in such and such a place." He knew that the world was less than perfect, but he thought the worst sufficiently documented, and his mission, as he saw it, was to bring people the best. Reflecting at the end of the Second World War on the mood of returning veterans, he said, "The atrocities and miseries will be difficult to forget. I know I can't give my Beautiful Italy lecture next session to men who know Italy only as a pigsty . . . One day these boys will forget and come to my lectures not to hoot but to relive the better moments and enjoy themselves."

When he retired in 1951, Burton Holmes had delivered over 8,000 lectures. By the time he died in 1958, television had taken over the job he had discharged so ardently for more than half a century. He taught generations of Americans about the great world beyond the seas. His books are still readable today and show new generations how their grandparents learned about a world that has since passed away but remains a fragrant memory.

THE WORLD 100 YEARS AGO

By Dr. Fred Israel

The generation that lived 100 years ago was the first to leave behind a comprehensive visual record. It was the camera that made this possible. The great photographers of the 1860s and 1870s took their unwieldy equipment to once-unimaginable places—from the backstreets of London to the homesteads of the American frontier; from tribal Africa to the temples of Japan. They photographed almost the entire world.

Burton Holmes (1870-1958) ranks among the pioneers who popularized photojournalism. He had an insatiable curiosity. "There was for me the fascination of magic in photography," Holmes wrote. "The word Kodak had not yet been coined. You could not press the button and let someone else do the rest. You had to do it all yourself and know what you were doing." Holmes combined his love of photography with a passion for travel. It didn't really matter where—only that it be exciting.

"Shut your eyes, tight!" said Holmes. "Imagine the sands of the Sahara, the temples of Japan, the beach at Waikiki, the fjords of Norway, the vastness of Panama, the great gates of Peking." It was this type of visual imagination that made Burton Holmes America's best known travel lecturer. By his 75th birthday, he had crossed the Atlantic Ocean 30 times and the Pacific 20, and he had gone around the world on six occasions. Variety magazine estimated that in his five-decade career, Holmes had delivered more than 8,000 lectures describing almost every corner of the earth.

Burton Holmes was born in Chicago on January 8, 1870. His privileged background contributed to his lifelong fascination with travel. When he was 16, his maternal grandmother took him on a three-month European trip, about which he later wrote:

> I still recall our first meal ashore, the delicious English sole served at the Adelphi Hotel [Liverpool] . . . Edinburgh thrilled me, but Paris! I would gladly have travelled third class or on a bike or on foot. Paris at last! I knew my Paris in advance. Had I not studied the maps and plans? I knew I could find my way to Notre Dame and to the Invalides without asking anyone which way to go. (The Eiffel Tower had not yet been built.) From a bus-top, I surveyed the boulevards—recognizing all the famous sights. Then for a panoramic survey of the city, I climbed the towers of Notre Dame, then the Tour St. Jacques, the Bastille Column, and finally the Arc De Triomphe, all in one long day. That evening, I was in Montmartre, where as yet there stood no great domed church of the Sacre Coeur. But at the base of the famous hill were the red windmill wings of the Moulin Rouge revolving in all their majesty. My French—school French—was pretty bad but it sufficed. Paris was the springtime of my life!

Holmes never lost his passion for travel nor his passion for capturing his observations on film. He has left us with a unique and remarkable record that helps us to visualize the world many decades ago.

Lecturing became Holmes's profession. In 1892-93 he toured Japan. He discovered that "it was my native land in some previous incarnation—and the most beautiful land I have known." Holmes had the idea of giving an illustrated lecture about Japan to an affluent Chicago audience:

> I had brought home a large number of Japanese cards such as
> are used in Japan for sending poems or New Year's greetings.
> They were about two inches by fourteen inches long. I had the
> idea that they would, by their odd shape, attract instant notice.
> So I had envelopes made for them, employing a Japanese artist
> to make a design.

Holmes sent about 2,000 invitations to the socially prominent
whose addresses he took from the *Blue Book*. He "invited" them
to two illustrated lectures at $1.50 each on "Japan—the Country
and the Cities." ($1.50 was a high sum for the 1890s considering
that the average worker earned about $1 per day.) Both perfor-
mances sold out.

Burton Holmes's "Travelogues" (he began using the term in
1904) rapidly became part of American upper class societal life.
Holmes engaged the best theater or concert hall for a week at a
time. His appearance was an annual event at Carnegie Hall in
New York, Symphony Hall in Boston, and Orchestra Hall in
Chicago. His uncanny instinct for exciting programs invariably
received rave reviews. Once he explained how he selected his
photographic subjects:

> If I am walking through Brussels and see a dog cart or some
> other unimportant thing that is interesting enough for me to
> watch it, I am totally certain others would be interested in seeing
> a photograph of it.

A conservative man, Holmes avoided political upheavals,
economic exploitation, and social conflicts in his travelogues.
"When you discuss politics," he said, "you are sure to offend."
Holmes focused on people, places, and customs. He offered his
audience a world which was unfailingly tranquil and beautiful.

In 1897, Holmes introduced motion picture segments into his
programs. ("Neapolitans Eating Spaghetti" was his first film
clip.) His engaging personality contributed to his success. His

crisp narrative was delivered in a pleasant and cultured tone. He always wore formal dress with striped pants before an audience. Holmes took pride in creating an atmosphere so that his listeners could imagine the "Magic of Mexico" or the "Frivolities of Paris." "My first ambition was to be a magician," he said. "And, I never departed from creating illusions. I have tried to create the illusion that we are going on a journey. By projecting the views, I tried to create the illusion we are looking through 'the window of travel' upon shifting scenes." Holmes's travelogues were immensely successful financially—and Holmes became one of history's most indefatigable travelers.

Holmes's lectures took place during the winter months between the 1890s and his retirement in the early 1950s. In between, he traveled—he crossed Morocco on horseback from oasis to oasis (1894); he was in the Philippines during the 1899 insurrection; in 1901, he traversed the Russian Empire, going from Moscow to Vladivostok in 43 days. He visited Yellowstone National Park (1896) before it had been fully mapped. He was always on the move, traveling to: Venice (1896); London (1897); Hawaii (1898); The Philippines (1899); Paris (1900); Russia, China, and Korea (1901-02); Madeira, Lisbon, Denmark, and Sweden (1902); Arizona, California, and Alaska (1903); Switzerland (1904); Russia and Japan (1905); Italy, Greece, Egypt, and Hong Kong (1906); Paris, Vienna, and Germany (1907); Japan (1908); Norway (1909); Germany and Austria (1910); Brazil, Argentina, and Peru (1911); Havana and Panama (1912); India and Burma (1913); the British Isles (1914); San Francisco (1915); Canada (1916); Australia and New Zealand (1917); Belgium and Germany (1919); Turkey and the Near East (1920); England (1921); China (1922); North Africa (1923); Italy (1924); Ceylon (1925); Holland (1926); France (1927); Spain (1928); London (1929); Ethiopia (1930); California (1931); Java (1932); Chicago (1933); the Soviet Union (1934); Normandy and Brittany (1935); South America (1936); South Africa (1937); Germany (1938).

Holmes's black and white photographs have extraordinary clarity. His sharp eye for the unusual ranks him as a truly outstanding photographer and chronicler of the world.

Holmes's lectures on the Panama Canal were his most popular—cities added extra sessions. For Holmes though, his favorite presentation was always Paris—"no city charms and fascinates us like the city by the Seine." He found Athens in the morning to be the most beautiful scene in the world—"with its pearl lights and purple-blue shadows and the Acropolis rising in mystic grandeur." Above all though, Japan remained his favorite land—"one can peel away layer after layer of the serene contentment which we mistake for expressionlessness and find new beauties and surprises beneath each." And Kyoto, once the capital, was the place he wanted most to revisit—and revisit. Holmes never completed a travelogue of New York City—"I am saving the biggest thing in the world for the last." At the time of his death in 1958 at age 88, Holmes had visited most of the world. He repeatedly told interviewers that he had lived an exciting and fulfilling life because he had accomplished his goal—to travel.

In a time before television, Burton Holmes was for many people "The Travelogue Man." He brought the glamour and excitement of foreign lands to Americans unable to go themselves. His successful career spanned the years from the Spanish-American War in 1898 to the Cold War of the 1950s—a period when Americans were increasingly curious about distant places and peoples. During this time period, travel was confined to a comparative handful of the privileged. Holmes published travelogues explaining foreign cultures and customs to the masses.

In this series of splendid travel accounts, Holmes unfolds before our eyes the beauties of foreign lands as they appeared almost a century ago. These volumes contain hundreds of photographs taken by Holmes. Through his narratives and illustrations we are transported in spirit to the most interesting countries and cities of the world.

PEKING

Burton Holmes visited Peking (now Beijing) in August 1901, two years after a Chinese society called *I Ho Ch'uan,* which means "Society of the Righteous, Harmonious Fists"—known to the West as the Boxers—had drawn the Western world's attention to this remote and mysterious capital of China.

The "Boxer Rebellion" was an attempt to purge China of Westerners and Western influence. The fiercely nationalistic and violent Boxers detested foreigners, Christian missionaries, and the continued territorial concessions made by some Chinese leaders to European nations. In late 1899, the Boxers began to burn Catholic churches and murder missionaries throughout eastern China.

Alarmed, the Peking diplomatic corps requested protection, and an international force of more than 2,000 marched to their assistance from the coastal city of Tientsin. China's Dowager Empress and her advisors considered this an invasion. The Boxers now began massacring foreigners, and they isolated Peking by cutting railway and telegraph lines. The Westerners in the city took refuge in the legation buildings, which were in a compact group. The Boxer siege of this compound lasted from the summer of 1899 through mid-August 1900. Future president Herbert Hoover, then a 26-year old mining engineer in China, wrote a harrowing account of this year, chronicling their dwindling food, water shortages, and genuine fear.

On June 10, 1900, an international army of about 16,000 troops with contingents from seven nations, including the United States, landed in Tientsin. On August 4, they reached Peking and lifted the siege of the compound. Within ten days, this army controlled Peking and the Chinese royal court fled the city.

What followed was one of the most hideous episodes in the history of East-West relations. An orgy of looting by foreigners began—soldiers and civilians, diplomats and missionaries plundered palaces and private homes. Unashamedly, they triumphantly carried off the spoils. On September 7, 1901, while Holmes was in Peking, the Western powers dictated the Boxer Protocol to the royal family. This harsh settlement involved a huge monetary indemnity ($24.5 million to the United States alone) as well as trade concessions to the European nations. Because China was unable to pay the complete amount, the European nations besieged customs stations until the protocol's terms had been fulfilled. In addition, the foreign legations in Peking were placed under international control, and this area was withdrawn from Chinese jurisdiction. Thus, a portion of Peking a few yards from the royal palaces became a foreign city. The aftermath of the Boxer Rebellion further contributed to Chinese distrust of the West, a distrust that has lasted throughout the 20th century.

Holmes's 1901 visit to China coincided with the end of the tumultuous Boxer Rebellion. Holmes has given us a unique view of Peking through both his text and his photographs. His description of Peking and its people, customs, and landmarks is a major contribution to the historic literature and helps us to understand the Chinese people as they were at the beginning of this century.

Peking

PEKING, capital of the Celestial Empire — fortified camp
of the Manchu conquerors — acres of dead magnificence
and living desolation, half hidden in a glorifying haze of incan-
descent dust — dominated by sixteen towering city-gates —
shut in by miles of jealous walls now breached and tunneled
for the invading locomotive — the troops of many nations
quartered in her sacred places — her innermost '' Forbidden
City '' become the playground of the curious — the palaces of
the absent '' Son of Heaven '' profaned and despoiled of their
empty mysteries — her population cowed and embittered,

regarding with mute defiance the exodus of tue avengers and the rebuilding of the fortress-like legations—this is the Peking of the year of Our Lord 1901.

Christendom at last made herself felt in China, but heroic as was her entrance upon the scene, her sojourn and retirement can be recalled by lovers of humanity with naught but

THE GULF OF PE-CHI-LI

regret. Attenuate it as you will, allow for the exaggerations of the press reports, the extravagances that the rolling story gathers as it travels from Orient to Occident, the fact remains that Western Civilization stands disgraced in the eyes of universal Justice. Foreign occupation has confirmed the Chinese in their belief that Western nations are barbarian

A glorious opportunity to give light and health and life to four hundred millions of our fellow-creatures was neglected by the enlightened powers, robbed of their initiative for good by selfish jealousies. True, the chastisement of China was imperative. China has been chastised. But how? Thousands of innocent folk have suffered; hundreds of peaceful villages have been destroyed; a few of the supposed guilty have been punished; but the actual instigators of the Boxer outbreak and the more powerful ones who supported and encouraged the fanatics still sit in high places, or, at the worst, loll in a luxurious exile. Christendom now abandons China burdened with debt, and officially invites the old régime to resume its blighting sway in the Forbidden City. The last state of the "Sick Man of Asia" is worse than the first.

I do not question for a moment the statement of an officer who said on leaving Peking in August, 1901, "It is not good-by. We shall all be back before long, the job is only patched up, it is not finished."

The story of the Boxer outbreak, of the siege of the legations, of the relief-expeditions, and of the capture and occupation of Peking by the international forces, has been already told a hundred times from a hundred points of view. In these pages we are to follow, merely as interested travelers, the route from Taku to Peking, to look upon the scenes made memorable by these events and other scenes that are significant because they throw a little light upon the problem of the East—the mystery of China.

As one evening early in August, 1901, we approach the Chinese coast, en route from Nagasaki to Taku, we see the sun of progress gilding the celestial skies. It is the

CHI-FU

same glorious orb that in its daily course has lighted up the
finished, splendid capitals of modern Europe, smiled upon the
new-born cities of the broad United States, glanced at fair
Honolulu, and marveled at the rapidly progressing cities of
Japan. It is now looking down upon the capital of China to
see what England, Germany, France, Italy, Austria, America, and Dai Nippon have accomplished, yonder in Peking,

OFF TAKU

in the name of humanity and progress. Our steamer touches
at Chi-fu, a busy port, picturesque, semi-European, abound-
ing in missionary schools and institutions, and foreign banks,
with the consulates of the great nations crowning the bluff,
and with ships from the four corners of the earth at anchor
in the spacious harbor which is alive with smaller native craft.

But at Chi-fu we shall not disembark. We steam on
westward all night across the gulf of Pe-chi-li, and find ourselves at sunrise off Taku, the famous port of Peking—a
long way "off Taku," for we are amid the warships at the
outer anchorage, so far from shore that we see nothing but

the sea, the sky, and that amazing archipelago of war-ships —the huge fleet of the Allied Powers. On all sides lie the sullen cruisers, the watch-dogs of Europe, crouching at this watery threshold of decrepit China. Nearly all the great powers are represented in this floating congress of avengers; but we have intercourse with

A CHINESE CRAFT

but one iron-clad, the flag-ship of the French, the "Rédoubtable." We accost her on washing-day, as is evidenced by the aspect of the yards, half concealed by the clothes of the crew hung out to dry. Had it not been for the courtesy of the French naval-officers (among whom was numbered Pierre Loti, author of "*Les Derniers Jours de Pékin*"), we should

have suffered great inconvenience in reaching shore. We arrive on a steamer chartered by the French government to carry mails from Nagasaki to the ships of the French squadron off Taku.

A JUNK

We travel on sufferance and without any assurance of being put ashore in China, for there are no tenders save the launches of the fleet, and the port is seventeen miles from the anchorage. Our only alternative would have been to hail one of the lazy fishing-junks, making their shoreward way to the slow dip of tired oars and the flapping of listless sails composed of heavy mats of straw. But fortunately we are spared the threatened six hours of that sort of thing; after some delay and four thrilling transfers in a rough sea, from

TRYING TRANSFERS

tugs to launches and from launches to an improvised tender, we finally go speeding over the yellow waves toward the celebrated mud forts of Taku. They rise, menacing and repellent, from a shore so low and featureless that it appears merely like a thick yellow scum lying upon the waters.

The forts are ponderous walls of yellow clay, raised to protect the entrance to yellow Pei-Ho River—and to be taken repeatedly by foreign foes. The initial act in a war with China is usually the taking of the Taku Forts. They served their purpose as well in 1900 as they did in 1861; that is, they fell at the proper moment but, it must be confessed, this was after a brief defense that cost the allies dear. Thereupon, however, the garrisons adhered so successfully to the tradition of

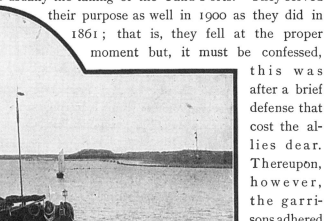

THE SOUTH FORTS AT TAKU

the Taku garrisons, that the war-correspondents could cable their papers to use the old line in stereotype, "The Chinese ran away." Between the forts the Pei-Ho River empties its soiled and dingy waters into the soiled and dingy yellow sea. We hear the epithet of "noble" applied so frequently to famous rivers that it is

THE NORTH FORT AT TAKU

almost a relief to find a stream which does not call for that most dignified of adjectives. The Pei-Ho is eminently an ignoble stream—a turbid, turgid canal of yellowish mud.

creeping in awkward curves between low slimy shores, which seem to be a portion of the ugly stream itself, solidified and raised a few feet above the general level.   The town of Taku on the right bank is one of the most hopeless places of human habitation I have ever seen.   Its houses are of yellow mud, its people of yellow clay, its streets appear like furrows in a plain of mud — the whole seems like some horrible haunt of amphibious maggots, uncovered by a sudden subsidence of

TAKU TOWN

the dirty waters.   Our hearts sink at the thought that fellow human-beings can exist in such a place.   Along the water-front, naked children are wading in the slime, where only a few months before had lain the myriad corpses that came drifting downstream to tell of the unspeakable horrors that attended the advance of the invaders.

A little way above that soggy village of Taku we see a trim white ship-of-war at anchor; it flies our flag; it is the veteran keel of Chinese waters, the antique of the United

States Navy, the antediluvian, "Monocacy." She was sent
out to die in China; but life is strong in the sturdy old craft,
and she will continue to spend her declining days at rest
upon the yellow tides of celestial rivers. She played no part
in the taking of the forts; but we need not discuss the pros
and cons of the commander's attitude. We know that it
was not want of pluck that kept her out of the initial row,
for later on she did the state much service in the shallow
upper reaches of the river near Tien-Tsin.

The Pei-Ho is alive with junks, all flying the flag of one
or another of the Allied Nations, or a banner bearing
the legend, "Licensed by the Provisional Government."
Foreign flags flutter protectingly above many of the hovels in

THE U. S. S. MONOCACY

the muddy wilderness of Taku. We are put on shore on the left bank, at a place that bears the name of Tongku. We wade through mud as deep as our disgust, following a long procession of coolies who have with pirate-like ferocity pos-

TONGKU

sessed themselves of our belongings. Tongku is not a pleasant place. There is an unsubstantiality about its thoroughfares that inspires a vague dread of sudden sinkings into an even more infernal region. It is with thankfulness that we find ourselves and our possessions safely housed in the Tivoli

Hotel which lies, I was about to say, within a few paces of the station; but, to be more exact, it lies within four mud-puddles and two refuse-heaps, of the railway-yard. To

PORTERS

our surprise, we find that in spite of all we are still hungry ; in fact, our appetites have waxed so strong that even Taku and Tongku cannot overcome them.   Accordingly we dine upon the best that the Tivoli can offer.   And here, even in this hopeless place, the genius of the Gallic race asserts itself, for the proprietor is a Frenchman, and the dinner that he provides is excellent,—well cooked and well served by a diminutive Celestial.   *Vive la cuisine Française!*

THE RAILWAY-STATION, TONGKU

Tongku is the starting-point of the railway-line to Peking. We find the line restored, and operated under the direction of the British.   The station-guards are Sikhs of the Hong-kong regiment ; the conductors are Australian man-of-war's men ; the ticket-takers are Chinese, and the station-master is an Englishman.   We know all this because the combined force turns out to arrest us.   We chance to be wearing our Russian military caps, bought in Blagoveschensk on our recent journey across Siberia.   The Russians and the British

had come almost to blows, a short time before, in a dispute about railway privileges and control. We are planting tripods and taking photographs. This arouses the suspicions of the Sikh sentry who reports that Russian agents are surveying the line. He is ordered to call the guard by the station-master, who meantime rushes out to remonstrate with us. Bitter is the chagrin of the Sikh who started the alarm, when it transpires that we are not minions of the Tsar and that we have no designs upon the transportation system of North China. While we are laughing over the discomforture of the zealous Indian, so jealous of British influence as opposed to Russian, a train comes rolling down from Peking with a regiment of Germans, in khaki uniform, with golden eagles in their helmets.

A SIKH

GERMANS

AT THE TONGKU STATION

The exodus of the Allies has begun. To-morrow they embark for Bremen ; but many of their officers will travel homeward via San Francisco and New York, studying the homeland of their greatest commercial rivals. Every hour there comes to this busy station a crowded train from some point up the line, bringing detachments of all sorts and conditions of soldiers, and usually a string of native pigtails long enough to reach from Tongku to Peking We start from Tongku in the late afternoon, ourselves in one of the bare, cool railway-carriages and our luggage in an ovenlike van made of metal, where it is placed in charge of a tall Sikh who represents the only checking-system operative in these disturbed days.

Toward sunset we approach Tien-Tsin, beyond which the evening train does not proceed. We have traversed about twenty-five miles of desolation in one hour and a half. Our train is filled with officers of half a dozen nationalities, and men of diverse

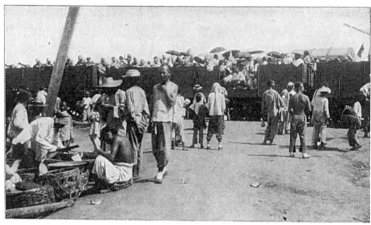

HUMAN FREIGHT

regiments, from the trim, well-groomed "Tommy Atkins" to the badly soiled soldiers of France and Italy; from the immaculate little Japanese, to the smelly, brawny Russians. Five lines of military telegraph parallel the railway, establishing instant communication between headquarters at Peking and every outpost of every nation along this highway now controlled by the military forces of the Allied Powers.

In Tien-Tsin we receive again that impression of unending toil — which is to me the first, the last, and the most enduring impression that I brought from China — toil that knows

NEARING TIEN-TSIN

no beginning, for it begins before the toilers have begun to think ; toil that never ceases, for without it there would be an end to life ; toil that racks muscles, tears flesh, fixes on every brow of bronze a crown of pearls of sweat ; toil that would be heroic were it not utterly unconscious of itself.

Well may we call the Chinese "ants," and their cities "ant-hills." The heel of Europe may crush and scatter the

TIEN-TSIN

heaps raised by these busy toilers, and grind out a million busy lives. It avails nothing. Other millions of toilers recommence the task, and build again — instinctively as ants — another city after their own fashion. The native city of Tien-Tsin, now in ruins, is policed by foreign troops. Its ramparts have been razed ; smooth boulevards have been created where useless city-walls once stood. The ants look on without wonder or complaint, and those who toil in

TIEN-TSIN TOILERS

transport choose the new unobstructed road made by the "foreign devil"; but never would they have made it for themselves. Left to themselves they will in time obliterate all traces of this foreign occupation, and forget the days when European and Japanese patrols marched through their streets, hindering the progress of the creaking wheelbarrows, the swinging baskets, and the green sedan-chairs of pompous mandarins.

Although it strikes us as an unfamiliar fact, we can accept without a question the statement that this city of

THE RUINED NATIVE CITY

Tien-Tsin is the second largest
in the empire; larger than
Peking, and smaller only
than Canton, the south-
ern metropolis. Esti-
mated roughly the re-
spective populations are,
Canton two million souls;
Tien-Tsin one million, and
Peking, the capital, once be-
lieved to be the most populous city

A SUNSHADE

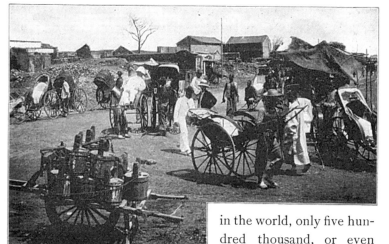

SITE OF THE DEMOLISHED CITY WALLS

in the world, only five hundred thousand, or even
less. Tien-Tsin was
the residence of Li Hung Chang during his long
viceroyship of the Province of Pe-chi-li. His
yamun is now occupied by the Provisional Government, and there we find the mess-table of the
hard-working, conscientious Europeans, who
in this critical time are ruling wisely and
justly the unnumbered millions of this
devastated province. But the "P. G.,"
as this provisional government is called,

MIDDAY REPOSE

knows China too well to alter the old ways—in the courtyard two Chinese policemen are "bambooing" a Chinese malefactor, to the obligato screeched by his protesting wife—and this is done by order of the all powerful "P. G."

An illustration of the Chinese way of doing

THE JAPANESE PATROL

things is afforded at one end of the bridge that spans the river at this point. There is a difference in the levels of street and bridge. No one has ever thought to ease the bump by the

DESOLATION IN TIEN-TSIN

YAMUN OF LI HUNG CHANG

placing of an inclined plank.   All day long the patient human
horses of Tien-Tsin waste their strength in butting at that
bump with rikishas, laden carts, and over-laden wheel-barrows.

In one sense, at least, much of the salt of the earth
is gathered at Tien-Tsin.   Although our officers and soldiers

IN THE YAMUN COMPOUND

merit well the title, I do not allude to General Chaffee and his men ; of them, and of their almost unique attitude of honesty during the period of international thieving, I shall not attempt to speak. I was not in China during those times of

PIGTAILED PRISONERS

THE OFFICIAL MESS IN THE VICEROY'S PALACE

confusion. I know only from hearsay what was done, and hearsay has it that Chaffee and our boys controlled by him were then

AT THE BRIDGE

about the only clean-handed folk in
China.   The salt I speak of is real
salt, mountains of it heaped upon
the banks of the Pei-Ho, each
saline sierra covered with
straw mats.   It is the tribute
salt,—the salt of the gov-
ernmental monopoly, one
of the chief sources of in-
come for the Imperial Ex-
chequer.

There are two cities of
Tien-Tsin, one Chinese and
the other international.   We

THE
ASTOR HOUSE
HOTEL

SALINE SIERRAS

A FERRY ON THE PEI-HO

lodge in the French quarter, where we sleep on the floor at one end of the hallway at the Hôtel des Colonies.   But although beds are dear and hard to find,—harder yet when

HÔTEL DES COLONIES

we do find them,— there is no lack of
cheap conveyances, as we discover
whenever we step to the door-
way to hail a rikisha man — a
veritable avalanche of rikishas
invariably descends upon us.

RIKISHA RIDING
IN TIEN-TSIN

Straight away from the end of
the *Rue* where the French quarter terminates, runs *Victoria Road*,
the chief thoroughfare of British Tien-Tsin. We have time

GORDON HALL

only for a glance at Gordon Hall, the municipal building,
memorable as the refuge for the foreign women and children
of Tien-Tsin during the siege,— a siege not one whit less trying than that experienced by the Peking legationers.   For
many days shells were falling in this foreign settlement,
dropping in at meal-time, making sunrise calls at the bedside,

or whizzing overhead like shrill messengers of terror, delivering with screeching emphasis the expressions of hatred sent by exasperated China to the despised "foreign devils."

The world knows how an end was put to that brief reign of terror—how Russian, Japanese, and British troops stormed and took the native city, then surrounded by its

THE AMERICAN CONSULATE AT TIEN-TSIN

formidable wall, while the ill-fated Ninth Infantry—fresh from a hard campaign in the Philippines was cut to pieces amid the marshes between the foreign quarter and the native town. We visit the spot where Colonel Liscum fell. Whose was the blame it will be difficult to say. A general of the Allies, directing the assault, ordered our men here with the

vague command, "Advance left or right, it makes no difference; but hurry!" It did make a difference—an
advance to the right was to prove fruitless and fatal.   But

WHERE THE NINTH REGIMENT WAS DECIMATED

the Ninth went to the right and to decimation in obedience
to the command. The walls and houses were alive with
Chinese sharpshooters, the marshy
ditches were too deep for ford-
ing; there was practically
no shelter, retreat was
impossible, and our
men were shot down,
hopelessly, miser-
ably, while the other
troops won glory at
the gates and on the
walls.

   From Tien-
Tsin to Pe-
king the dis-
tance is about

RAILWAY-STATION, TIEN-TSIN

A PEI-HO HOUSEBOAT

seventy-five miles.   We cover it in five hours in a comfort-
able train.   Formerly the usual mode of travel to Peking was

AN OBSERVATION-CAR

LANG-FANG STATION

by junk or house-boat "tracked" up the muddy Pei-Ho by
a gang of coolies, the voyage demanding several days. Our
Chinese fellow-travelers in the flat-cars are not the least

RECOVERING SUBMERGED RAILS

A WANDERING MINSTREL

interesting feature of the trip; packed in by hundreds, they yet maintain a certain poise and dignity peculiar to the Oriental, even under the most adverse conditions. All foreheads are closely shaven, all pigtails neatly braided, and every man has his sun-hat, his sunshade, or his fan.

At every station we are reminded of the wave of destruction that swept along this line as almost the first indication of the coming Boxer storm. The buildings are mere shells, with roofs and windows eaten by the flames. It was at one of these stations that Admiral Seymour was compelled to give up hope of reaching Peking by rail. Bridges were down and rails were up, and the relief expedition abandoned the train and started on its disastrous

VENDERS

THE TEMPLE OF HEAVEN TERMINAL

march toward the capital. It was turned back by weight of Chinese numbers and European wounded. But the Chinese are paying for the havoc wrought and for the sufferings endured by the victims of their rage.

We see large bands of ex-Boxers toiling waist-deep in the slimy pools along the line,—diligently bringing to light the English rails which they had so gleefully flung down from the embankment a few short months before. During the long stops at the ruined stations we study with interest the crowds of native venders—men and boys from the neighboring villages who are recouping their personal losses by selling fruit and bottles of beer or mineral water. Many of them

ARRIVAL AT PEKING

also jingle handfuls of silver ten-cent pieces, crying, "changee dollar, changee dollar!" and to our surprise they gladly give eleven Japanese dimes for every Japanese or Chinese silver dollar! The Chinese regard only the bullion value of precious metals—they know full well that there is more silver in one big dollar than in eleven little dimes.

We roll from station to station, each one more miserable than the last, on across the fields of towering maize or sorghum stalks with the five parallels of telegraph poles to keep

PEKING!

us company, until after five hours of interesting monotony, there rises before us—as suddenly as if it had been thrust up from the earth—the great South Gate of Peking. The west end of its curving roof is partially wrecked; otherwise the portal is intact, and to right and left stretch the mighty walls of the Chinese city. But the train does not even hesitate at sight of the frowning walls; to our amazement it rolls on as if in a revengeful fury it would batter down that range of medieval masonry, behind which has always lurked so much of ignorant pride and supercilious superiority. We

brace ourselves for the expected shock of collision ; — but no
shock comes.   Again we lean far out and look ahead ; and
looking we see that which our generation scarcely hoped to
see — a locomotive rolling triumphantly through the breached
walls of the Celestial Capital ! The isolation of Peking
is ended ; that breach will never be blocked.   It does but
figure the deep cut in China's national pride — a cut that
never will be healed.   With a loud shriek of joy the locomotive sweeps proudly across the vacancies of Peking's great

ALLIED OFFICERS ARRIVING IN THE EMPEROR'S PRIVATE CAR

southern plaza — an enormous waste place so broad and long
as to appear like a suburban wilderness, belted by walls,
blotched with miry ponds, and glorified by a flood of sun-
shine, pure and dazzling above, but, near the ground, yel-
lowed and actinically attenuated by that wonderful dust-sea
in which Peking appears to be submerged to the depth of
three or four feet.   A moment more and our train halts at
a platform before the very gate to the Temple of Heaven
converted for the moment into a railway terminal station !
Think of it ! The unapproachable, inviolable Temple of
Heaven, defiled by the smoky breath of the Iron Horse.

Any doubts that we are really in Peking are set at rest by a signboard,—bearing the word "Pekin"—to which we take exceptions because the pronunciation of the name calls for a final "G." It is Pe-king' and not Pee'kin, the railway-company to the contrary notwithstanding. Still, the railway administration should certainly be well qualified linguistically, for another interesting signboard tells us the "Railway Staff

THAT ALL MAY READ

Officer" must not only answer to his title in English, he must also know that he is "*Eisenbahn Stabs Offizier,*" "*Officier de l'État Major de Chemin de Fer,*" "*Jelyezno Dorojnaya Staonie Ofizter,*" "*Ufficiale Capo Statione,*" and several other things, in Japanese, Chinese, and Hindustanee. And all these various tongues are not glued to the printed board, they are wagging wildly in the mouths of the mixed multitude assembled at the station, the polyglot chorus dominated by the endless and persistent sing-song of Celestial speech — interrupted only by grunts of pain as the stick of a British-Indian sentry falls on the bare bony back of some too eager native.

Sons of the Heavenly Empire have meantime seized our twenty-seven boxes, cameras, and tripods, and are now engaged in solving the Chinese puzzle, — how to stow them all into two Peking carts.

The Peking cart has furnished many an amusing chapter in tales of Chinese travel, but although we have had our first

A PEKING CART

impressions of it discounted by description, we find it still, as it has always been, one of the wonders of the earth — and it is of the earth earthy, despite its sky-blue canopy. Its favorite garb is mud, its best-loved haunts the ruts of hopeless roads — its sole ambition, to show how far over it can lurch without capsizing, and its only pride, its indestructibility. Only the Pekingese know how to enter into and enjoy the Peking cart. Foreigners find it impossible to get aboard without instruction or example, such as is furnished us by a lady of the Manchu clan, who may be seen in the frontispiece. She gracefully glides in, stepping up, turning, sitting, and then sliding backwards on the inclined floor to a position just above the springless axle. She sits there, tailor fashion, her children on either side—her lord and master taking up his position where one shaft joins the body of the

GOING UP TOWN

cart, while the driver perches on the other shaft, whence he can prod the mule at his ease and dangle his feet in the dust cloud raised by the yellow wheels.

The point of view enjoyed by the passenger is more or less peculiar, as will be proved by a glance at a picture made while sitting cross-legged under the arching canopy of my first Peking cart. To me the mule looked more like a kangaroo; it even appeared to make tremendous leaps, but this

THE PASSENGER'S POINT OF VIEW

was an illusion caused by the sudden droppings of the cart into the cracks or mudholes. Then, too, the passing panorama, framed by the awning and the mule, gave me much the same impression as a very jerky motion-picture projected by a shaky cinematograph — this effect is due to the cruelly continued jolting of the cart, painful not only to the eyes, but to every fiber of the foreigner. For the Peking cart is absolutely springless, and the Peking pavement resembles the débris of an avalanche. It seems as if the cart itself were imbued with the spirits of ten thousand Boxers; it boxes you up, it boxes you down, it gives you upper cuts and

JINRIKISHAS

A BRIDGE

left-handers, knock-out blows and general punishment, and every blow as if by Boxer magic seems to attain the solar plexus. One's first trip in a Peking cart is a veritable voyage of discovery,—discovery of unsuspected kinks in one's own mortal coil. But seriously, the initial experience is attended by actual pain ; so rough are the pavements and so racking the jolts of the springless car of Juggernaut. I made attempts to soften the shocks by riding on the hands, thus lifting the body from the floor, but in vain ; every now and then up comes the floor, giving the shrinking passenger a blow that more than compensates for all the little shocks to which he has managed to rise superior. It is not possible to rise with success to

POLICE

the trot of this two-wheeled mustang. The victim crawls out from the Peking cart, stiff, racked, and riven, but rich in a new experience of which he is reminded every time he lifts a hand or moves a foot, or sits or rises or tries to turn

the head.   Forewarned of this, we deferred the experience
just described until our last day in Peking, and wisely took
jinrikishas, recently introduced, for the long ride to the hotel.
We formed almost a caravan, three rikishas for ourselves, one
for a British soldier who had volunteered to guide us, one for the
cameras and breakables, and two carts for the heavy baggage.

The Peking streets are either submerged in a sea of mud
or buried in a Sahara of yellow dust.   We find them an

CHIEN-MEN STREET

unhappy combination of bog and ash-heap.   "Indescrib-
able" is the word that best describes one's first impressions
of Peking ; other words that help a little are "bigness,"
"busy-ness," "desolation," and "dirt."   Signs of the
times are seen on every side,—the "signs" are in English
and German, and refer to soda-water, beer, and cigars.

The main thoroughfare, the Chien-men Street—bisects
the Chinese City from south to north, from the South Gate,

where the railway enters, to the Chien-men, the principal
gate in the wall separating the Chinese from the Tatar City.
This gate, once one of the most famous and familiar features
of Peking, is now in ruins. The formidable lower walls are
still intact, but the elaborate superstructure, with its red
pillars and its great roofs of tile, was swept away by the fire
started by the Boxers in the adjacent commercial quarter,

RUINS OF THE CHIEN-MEN

the rich shops of which were pillaged during the confusion.
Thus the most conspicuous landmark of Peking presents an
unfamiliar and significant aspect to the arriving traveler.
The Chien-men is in fact two gates, separated by a busy
court ; but ere we enter it, our progress is impeded for a
moment by the opposing stream of Peking traffic — so Asiatic
and so picturesque. Only the magic of the motion-picture
can reveal the peculiar fascination of the scene. The

camels, carts, and wagons filled with tribute rice having filed by and disappeared in that low-lying haze of golden dust, we pass through the first archway and find ourselves in the broad court between the gates, where surrounded by gigantic walls lies the busiest of all the busy cross-roads of Peking, the whole wonderful scene enveloped in a deeper, denser, more tawny flood of Peking dust.

Signs of the times again on every side ; above us is the ruined tower of the gate, where gallant Reilly fell while shelling the Imperial City ; on the left we see a little railway-car belonging to the Emperor's private train, in which he used to go careering round the gardens of the Winter Palace. It stands now in this common court as a shelter and resort for common folk. It would not be here had it not proved to be one of the rare lumps of loot that were too bulky for successful abstraction from the city. Through the second arch we make our way, strange sights calling our gaze in all directions ; then turning to the

THE PASSING THRONG

right we find ourselves in Legation Street.   It is a trim, well-
ordered, and official-looking avenue, strangely un-Pekingese.

What foreigner can look upon that thoroughfare without
emotion ?   For sixty days it held the anxious attention of the
world.   The gaunt forms of Death, Torture, and Horrors
Unspeakable strode up and down that avenue, then isolated
—cut off from the world as thoroughly as if it had been

A FUNERAL CORTÈGE

swallowed up by the flood of barbarism that was beating with
cowardly fury round the walls of the legations.

A mile dash over the new, smooth pavement of this
resuscitated street and a turn to the left brings us into the
Ha-Ta-men Street, where we are crowded into the ditch by
a funeral procession ; but this we do not resent, for the procession is spectacular and worthy of the right of way, and
the ditch leads to our hotel.   The only hotel in Peking,
in 1901, was the Hôtel du Nord, established soon after the

occupation of the city, by a German, who had brought his crockery, supplies, bed-clothes, and "boys" from Tien-Tsin on a fleet of fourteen river-junks, in the wake of the Allied Armies. The proprietor himself is on the threshold rebuking a drunken German soldier who has just smashed two jinrikishas after brutally kicking the coolies, because, in fear, they had refused to serve him — knowing from experience

HÔTEL DU NORD

that their only pay would come in the form of kicks. Similar occurrences were pitifully common.

The entrance to the new caravansary is not Waldorf-Astorian in splendor. In fact, the courts and buildings now occupied by the hotel were formerly the precincts of a pawn-shop. The German hotel-man was saved the trouble of moving out the pledges — the noble army of international looters looked to it that nothing of consequence should be

left to litter the apartments of the future Hôtel du Nord.
But we find the old traffic in brocades, bronzes, and cloi-
sonnés proceeding merrily in the first court, where merchants
gather every day to sell to tourists rare old curios, their
manifolded values justified by the whispering of the magic
but misleading word "loot." There is little good loot left
in Peking. Look for it in Bond Street and Fifth Avenue.

The rambling groups of low, one-story buildings that serve
as sleeping-rooms are scattered round about what looks like
a small vacant lot or courtyard,—called a "compound."

To cross that "compound"at night requires careful pre-
liminary calculations, for there are no lights to guide us
between the slimy little lakes and the hills of empty bottles,
or past the logs and carts and rubbish with which the

" LOOT "

THE HOTEL " COMPOUND "

monotony of the compound ·is diversified. These are, however, matters of no moment to us ; we come from comfortless Siberia. Moreover, the cuisine is marvelously good,
well worth the four gold-dollars charged per day ; and our
rooms, or rather, separate little houses, ranged about a
brick-paved, mat-roofed court, are fairly clean and comfort-
able, though at times damp enough to merit the epithet
"soggy." As for the service, there is no end to it.
"Boys " of all ages flit by dozens past our doors, carrying
water for the Anglo-Saxon tubs, polishing military boots and
chalking canvas shoes, pressing and repairing clothes, and hus-
tling tardy laundry-men. One is well waited upon in China.

Being at last housed in tolerable comfort, having dined
excellently well, the fatigues and cares of arrival are forgotten, and there comes the imperative desire to sally forth
to see in what manner of a city we are, and in what quarter
thereof we are lodged.

In the confusion and excitement of our hurried ride from
the station to the hotel, we had noted little save the oppres-
sive distances and the all-pervading dust. The streets of
Peking demand a chapter to themselves. The chapter
should be written with a fountain-pen that would flow mud,
and trace disgusting characters upon such crumpled scraps or

OUR ROOMS AT THE HÔTEL DU NORD

rags as would be rejected by the picker, and then the dust,
born of the mud, should be sprinkled on to blot the writing
lest it tell too much. The main streets that stretch from
gate to gate are as broad and dusty as deserts, or as wide
and wet as oceans, according to the weather. The narrow
intervening alleys are usually nothing more than fetid ditches.

Our first experience of Peking streets was such as to impress itself forever on the memory. We had arrived in the late afternoon by the comparatively smooth and well-traveled streets that lead from the railway terminus to the legation quarter. The night came on darker than pitch before we had time to venture out in search of first impressions. Peking was new to us, and we could not sleep until

A PEKING PUDDLE

we had made more intimate acquaintance with its thoroughfares, and sniffed its oriental smells. "But no one ever ventures out at night," they tell us. "Why?—is it dangerous?" we ask. "No; there is not the slightest danger. The Chinese are completely cowed; but there is absolutely no place for you to go; the city is dead, and the streets are

empty, unlighted, and impassable." "Splendid!" we
exclaim ; "no danger and no lights ; no people. Peking by
night all to ourselves! Magnificent!"

Accordingly we order three rikishas, three men to every
rikisha, and set out to cross the silent savage city and present
our letters of introduction to one of the missionaries of the

THE HA-TA GATE

American Board whose address is so remote and so indefinite
as to give to our projected outing the character of an explor-
ing expedition into the depths of darkest Peking.

It is impossible to suggest by means of pictures made by
day the impressions of that ride across Peking by night in
utter darkness. Despite the superficial dustiness, we find

A THOROUGHFARE

that recent rains have rendered the streets almost impassable. At first our human horses found a little terra firma by
hugging the walls, where at least one wheel would find a
track, while the other wheel was lifted by the perspiring

RUTS

helpers over abysses that looked bottomless. I state it as a sworn fact that several times when it became necessary to cross the street, we dared not attempt to do so until a man had been sent out with *a sounding-pole* to discover if there were a practicable ford across the thoroughfare at that point! To prove that this is not a too fantastic statement, one of the pictures shows the difference in level between the middle and the side of one of those streets. Imagine the upper road reduced to a ridge of almost fluent mud, as it would be in wet weather,—and the lower channel flooded as it is invariably after a heavy rain,—and you will agree that the *navigation* of the Peking streets by night is not without its difficulties and dangers. And then the bumps!—the ups and downs encountered even on the firmer border-strip that serves as sidewalk, and is usurped by the rikisha coolies.

THE WALKING IS WET

Imagine hovering in a rickety two-wheeled chair, in the blackness of night, on the brink of a mud-hole that may be bottomless for all that you can see—for as a rule you cannot see at all. Sometimes the rikisha drops squarely on two wheels with a sharp jolt on firm level ground; sometimes it sinks in yielding clay up to the axle; sometimes one tire strikes a rock and the other splashes into a pool of slimy ooze, from which the passenger is saved as if

AN ADVENTUROUS RIKISHA

by miracle, the coolies plunging in up to their knees and "boosting" the vehicle along until dry land is gained. These are not extraordinary incidents. We stopped counting similar hair-breadth escapes long before we reached our destination, which was the "*Fu*" or palace occupied by the American Board of Foreign Missions. The houses formerly occupied by the agents of the board had been of course destroyed by the Boxers, as one of the preliminaries of the

MUD

outbreak—the missionaries and their native converts taking refuge with the other foreigners in the legations.

MISSION OF THE AMERICAN BOARD

THE BUDDHA OF THE LAMA TEMPLE

We knocked repeatedly at the unlighted, temple-like portal of the Fu. At last an old Chinese appears, lantern in hand. We gather that the man we seek is not within; but as we turn to go, a cheery voice hails us, and from out the darkness of the street comes Mr. Stelle, returning from an evening visit to another mission. A long, intensely interesting talk of

BUDDHIST PRIESTS

recent misfortunes, struggles, and victories and of noble plans for nobler future battles with ignorance — then a return voyage in our jinrikisha, as eventful as the first.

We visited a few days later the site of the annihilated mission. There we found heaps of gray brick — all that remains of the many costly and commodious buildings. Who can blame the men who have seen the results of their life-labors reduced thus to heaps of charred and broken brick, for taking possession of the neighboring palace of a Tatar Prince, who was one of the chief instigators and backers of the Boxer movement? It is but justice that those who have lost all through the criminal connivance of the princes with the lawless element, should be sheltered by the very roof beneath which schemes were hatched for the

AT THE TEMPLE OF CONFUCIUS

WITH " LILY FEET "

destruction of the "foreign devil." Meantime the princely
owner of the palace is traveling "for his health" in the remote
interior provinces. We hear it often urged against missionary efforts, that China has a religion of her own, suited
to her people,—that foreigners should not interfere with
their beliefs. As for Buddhism, in the abstract it is beautiful
—but to what depths of degradation is it not sunk in the
Celestial Empire? There it is represented by a horde of
ignorant, filthy priests, droning in the dilapidated temples,
looking with hungry eyes at the inquisitive foreigners whom
they pursue with savagely insistent demands for offerings of
money. Playing upon the abject superstition of a populace

more ignorant than themselves, these shaven-pated Lamas are among the curses of the land. If one would be convinced of the utter demoralization of the priesthood of Gautama's faith, let him visit, as we did, the great Lama Temple in the far northeastern corner of the Tatar City, and study there the inane, vicious visages of the "holy men." It is like entering the haunt of birds of prey—now frightened into harmlessness, but retaining all the instincts of the vulture and the buzzard. Within the temple a Buddha—big as the Jupiter of the Acropolis—rises in its disdainful immensity above the petty thievery and fraud committed in his sacred name—a new curl of disdain added to his almost supercilious lip by

MANCHU WOMEN

the memory of recent depredations practiced by the invading Christians, who have carried off innumerable artistic knickknacks from his shrine. But even those who have no sympathy with mission-work confess that Buddhism has betrayed her trust in China—that Taoism has sunk to the level of fetish-worship, and that Confucianism is not and never has been more than an influence, tending at first to a higher life, but now become the chief impediment to the intellectual emancipation of four hundred million people. If one would know that there is no life in things Confucian, let him visit as we did the abandoned Temple of the Great Sage, and feel the chill of death that broods in those somber and forgotten courts. Even the irreligious must admit that China needs a new religion if only as *a means of escape* from the thralldom of tradition.

A cruel thralldom it is, that of Chinese tradition. One of the most painful proofs is—the martyred feet of Chinese women. Revolting to the foreign eye, the so-called "Lily

"COME AWAY, CHILDREN"

Feet'' are deemed both beautiful and fashionable by four
hundred million Asiatics.　What matter the sufferings of the
child?—her baby feet wrapped in the crippling bandages
during the years of growth,—bandages that are folded
tighter month by month as the violated little foot strives to
assert its rights to live and grow—making childhood one
long martyrdom of intense, never-remitting agony?　What
matter the inability of the crippled woman to move without
a twinge of pain?　She is a Chinese woman, and Chinese

A PEEP-SHOW

women must have "Lily Feet."　The very walk of the Lily
Footed lady—a stilted, uncertain toddle—betrays the
suffering resulting from a simple promenade.　Some cannot
walk at all without a cane.　And in this cruel custom she
persists, despite the good example set by her sisters of the
Manchu race, the wives and daughters of the conquering
Mongols who subjugated China three centuries ago, imposed
the pigtail on the men but did not take the bindings from the
feet of women.　A Manchu woman is distinguishable not

only by her big natural feet, shod almost like the feet of men, but also by her curious coiffure, a fanciful arrangement of the hair rivaling in fantastic outline the capillary architecture of the Japanese mousmé or of the maiden of Moki Land.

Impression-gathering in the Peking streets is a delightful occupation. I cannot conceive of anybody being bored in Peking. For him who has eyes to see and ears to hear and a nose to smell there is, in the language of the continuous-

A PAILOW NEAR THE CHIEN-MEN

vaudeville advertisements, "something doing every minute." The common, continuous passing throng is in itself enough to hold the attention for hours at a time; and to vary its marvelous monotony of brown body, blue trousers, and upheld paper fan, there are the vehicles, of many sorts— the low carts laden high with military supplies, drawn by small ponies, driven by half-nude teamsters; the familiar, but ever-astonishing passenger-cart, with its blue arched roof, its taut-stretched awning, shielding mule and driver, and its yellow wheels, tired with corrugated metal and thus equipped for the eternal task of filing deep grooves in the Peking pavements for other wheels to deepen, until the stones be cut in twain, and the roadway reduced to the Chinese ideal of what a road should be ("good for ten years and bad for ten thousand," runs the proverb) ; the frail jinrikishas, modern competitors of the perennial carts, with their

A BRIDAL-CHAIR

unhappy passengers, swaying and clutching at nothing as the bare-torsoed runners pull and propel the quivering vehicle over the rutted granite-blocks and through the abysmal puddles ; the ambulances of the foreign armies, trim, well-equipped and, by contrast, stylish, serving as carriages of state for the commanders ; the loud-voiced native wheel-barrows, squealing their woful song, uttering the mortal complaint of the poor dumb human brutes who push them : —

all these wheeled things go by as we stand watching and
watching beneath one of those strange street arches known
as "*pailows*," memorial structures erected in honor of some
great or good personage of whom we never heard.   Nor is
this all, for in that ever-passing river of unfamiliar things, we
now and then distinguish awkward dust-colored masses,
moving slowly, rhythmically — they are the ships of the Asian
deserts, fuller-rigged apparently than those of Africa, for the
Mongolian camels are shaggy as lions.   Then suddenly a

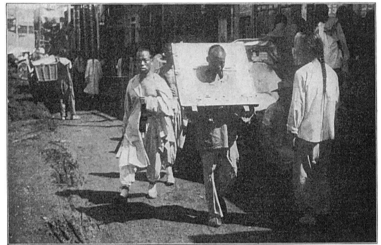

WORKING OUT A SENTENCE

glare of scarlet flashes in the crowd — it is a bridal-chair,
borne swiftly toward the house of some expectant bride-
groom, by carriers in festal garb ; or, again, it is the somber
green of an official chair, the equipage of one of the few
princes left in Peking to parley and make peace with the
intruders ; or, turning once more to those who pass on foot,
we see a miserable man wearing about his neck the heavy
wooden collar of the criminal, which frames his haggard
face, while upon it are pasted written papers, relating his
offense.   Meantime the uniforms of seven allied nations add
spots of red and blue and khaki to the kaleidoscopic crowd ;

and finally, to give a comic climax to it all, there dashes past the one unique conveyance of Peking, the contrivance of a foreign private soldier—a pony harnessed to a rikisha! and in Occidentalized Orientalism, that ingenious lad in khaki threads the maze of Peking—looking for all the world like a Norwegian peasant in a cariole!

The street life of Peking being so fascinating and dramatic a spectacle, it would seem a waste of time and money to patronize the theater. Yet we found it well worth while, if only for the sight of the half-nude audience perched on the

IN THE THEATER

comfortless seats—narrow benches without backs, no more luxurious than a string of carpenter's horses. But the Celestial has at least a few good practical ideas; he is sensible enough to take off his loose and scanty clothing when he attends the theater, while we put on our tightest and most cumbersome apparel. The play may be the thing—but in Peking as in the San Francisco China-town, noise is the only

thing distinguishable to the dazed foreigner ; the din of gongs
and cymbals is so loud and thick that one can almost *see* it.

From tragedy upon the stage we may turn in our swift
shifting of Oriental scenes, to the passing of a spectacular
funeral-procession. The hired mourners and attendants,
arrayed in soiled and tawdry finery, carrying gay parasols

IN TAWDRY FINERY

and baldachins and banners, precede what looks to us at
first like a compact group of football players in the throes
of a protracted struggle. It is, however, only what is best
described as a "gang" of pall-bearers, working in two
shifts, for the coffin under which they struggle weighs more
than a piano and the streets through which they advance so
painfully are, when good, more than ankle-deep in mud,
and when bad, bottomless. Were they to drop their burden,
a premature interment would take place then and there!

One of the pleasantest of our experiences in Peking was our brief acquaintance with Mr. I. C. Yang, a Chinese gentleman. Mr. Yang, as the sign before his door announces, is a manufacturer of aërated waters. He is also proprietor of the largest general foreign-goods store in the Tatar City. We were introduced to this progressive manufacturer and merchant by the commander of the American

THE PALL-BEARERS

guard, whom Mr. Yang had served as interpreter on several occasions during the critical period just closing. He speaks English perfectly. In talking with him we forget his nationality, and speak to him of "the Chinese" and "the natives," as if Mr. Yang himself were of our race, not theirs. He is one of the few Orientals who seem to understand the Occidental point of view. He devoted several days of his valuable time to showing us about the town. His cart and

saddle-horses were at our disposal, his servants ran errands
for us, and when he had not time to go with us, he sent an
intelligent interpreter who "rikishawed" with us and talked
for us as willingly and enthusiastically as an old friend. We
had but to express our desire to see or do a given thing, and
arrangements were made at once. Do we care to investigate
a pawnshop? Mr. Yang is stockholder in one of the most

AN ELABORATE CATAFALQUE

prominent loan-establishments, and we are invited to take
tea with the managing directors, in whose office we experience for the first time some of the curious forms of Chinese
hospitality. Arriving hot and dusty from the glaring streets,
our host greets us with a steaming towel, freshly wrung out
in hot water, which we press to our faces, finding much comfort in this kindly custom. After the towel has made the
complete round, tea is brewed in beautiful porcelain cups

with covers on, the covers being used to hold back the leaves as we sip the fragrant infusion. Wedges of water-melon are then driven into what remains of our thirst, and finally, being thoroughly refreshed, we are escorted to the court, or compound, where the choicest articles belonging to our Chinese "uncles" have been spread out for our inspection. We select a few distingués snuff-bot-tles of jade, crystal, or cornelian, —all of them quaintly beautiful, but none of them quite equal to one that had caught our fancy in the office. We ask its price and find that it is price-less, for the owner refuses to sell it, but at the same time

MR. YANG

A PROSPEROUS PAWN-SHOP

reiuses to let us go away without it—he forces it upon us as a gift! The temptation was too great—we accepted it.

Then follows an invitation to dine at the best surviving restaurant in town; I say "surviving" because few of the fashionable establishments lived through the siege. There for the first time in our lives we eat a complete Chinese dinner. It was a revelation; new flavors, new gastronomic sensations; a cuisine utterly unlike our own, but no less highly developed—no less indicative of culinary skill, experience, and genius. I cannot tell you what we ate—perhaps it

HOSPITALITY

would not sound quite appetizing; in fact, we did not ask —we were content that nearly every dish was novel and delicious. I tasted here the most exquisite meat-flavor that has ever appealed to my palate. It was associated with a dainty slice of mutton, streaked with fat, but so much more

THE PROPRIETORS

delicious than any meat morsel I had ever eaten that it seemed as if I were tasting some new, unknown kind of food. The secret of its preparation I could not learn. We ate, of course, with chop-sticks, long wands of ebony ; to clean them there were paper napkins, three inches square. Innumerable courses were brought on in confusing continuity. We tried one strange creation of the Chinese chef after another, and then went back to the beginning of the menu for "just one more " walnut fried in sugar, and one more lotus-bulb, or slice of pickled egg. As beverages there were hot tea and warm rice-wine, the latter poured from heavy pewter pots in form like tea-pots. To our surprise we lived to digest the dinner and tell the tale—and to regret that Celestial culinary skill should be handicapped by a disregard of cleanliness that would have shocked us had we not been fresh from the unwashed table-services of Siberia.

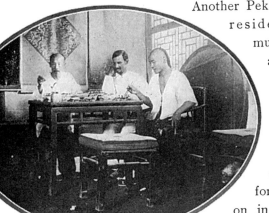

ESE DINNER

Another Pekingese—a temporary resident—who shows us much kindly courtesy is a well-known correspondent whose dispatches to the Associated Press and Reuter's Agency keep the English-speaking world informed of what is going on in Peking. He has adapted a Chinese house of the middle-class to the needs of a fastidious bachelor, and dwells amid his books and papers, quietly, as behooves the man

THE ASSOCIATED PRESS

whose profession is to listen to history as it is made, and to
transmit what comes into his ears to expectant millions—
who discuss it over their morning coffee on the other side of
the globe.   Despite the fact that Peking boasts the oldest
daily paper in the world, the official *Peking Gazette,*

PROCLAMATION BY THE FOREIGN DEVILS

local journalism does not appear to be flourishing.   The
newspapers of Peking are found upon the walls in the form
of placards—the latest proclamation being a warning from
the new governor to those who are attempting to reawaken
animosities, just as the late unpleasantness is drawing to a
close.   "Whereas," it read, "foolish men have stirred up

strife and attacked the foreigners, calamities have been brought upon our people, therefore refrain, etc.'' But the proclamation that will be longest remembered was the one posted by the Allies after the occupation of the city. For the first time in the history of the capital, the Pekingese were addressed directly and authoritatively in the name of the government of the despised foreign devils. This extraordinary proclamation related to the Pekingese in very

GATE-HOUSE OF THE AMERICAN LEGATION

moderate and sober terms how they had been wicked, wrought havoc, and brought punishment upon themselves ; it informed them that foreign troops would occupy their city until tranquillity should be restored, and it warned them that any future indiscretions would be even more severely dealt with. These historic posters were printed in the ordinary

THE OFFICIAL CART

Chinese fashion from a large wood block on which the complicated characters are cut by hand. The impressions are taken laboriously by pressing big sheets of paper upon the sculptured board which has been smeared with ink.

If there be one place in Peking that interests us more than another, it is the Legation of the United States. As we

THE WATER-GATE THROUGH WHICH THE FIRST OF THE RELIEF FORCE ENTERED

approach the gate-house, we note with interest the significant
cuts and scratches made so recently by Chinese bullets.   But

GATE-HOUSE OF THE BRITISH LEGATION

little damage was done here, for, as is indicated by the horizontal slashes in the brick and mortar, the hail of lead came from right and left, from the barricades thrown up by the Boxer assailants at the extremities of Legation Street.

In fact, in August, 1901, one year after the siege, there is little to remind us of that period of terror. Legation-life goes on as calmly and luxuriously as of yore. Even the women do not hesitate to ride abroad in the official pea-green cart. Peking is daunted, the Boxers are forgotten, and, for the present, to be a white man or woman is to command respect, and to inspire fear — in fact, to be almost a god in the eyes of the disgruntled natives, who have had at last a lesson that has made an indelible impression.

WALL OF THE BRITISH LEGATION

We can scarcely realize that a few months before, the courtyard of our legation, where we now stroll about with one
who was "among those present," was under almost con-
tinual fire. Had not the gallant little band of defenders, led
by Meyers, taken and held the section of the Tatar Wall
immediately in the rear of the legation, the place would have
been untenable. Our minister, Mr. Conger, was one of the

A PEKING CARAVANSARY

towers of strength and courage during that awful period.
One of the women who lived through the siege assured us
that a word and a smile from Mr. Conger did the hungry
defenders as much good as a beefsteak, that his cheery com-
ments used to make palatable even the polo-pony cutlets and
other war-time table luxuries. We found that people in
Peking who know and value Mr. Conger were amazed at the
criticism directed against him by a portion of the press at home.

PROCLAMATIONS

Although the American Legation was never abandoned to the Boxers, its inmates took refuge in the British compound, which was surrounded by a stouter wall. Moreover, the British Legation was more commodious; it was farther from the city gates where the Chinese guns were mounted, and it fronted on a canal which served it as a moat. A glance at one corner of that improvised fortress shows how severely it suffered from the effects of shot and shell. Sandbags still lie thick on the top of the wall, telling of the defensive industry of the besieged—and there upon the seared and riven wall some thoughtful survivor of the siege has traced the words, "Lest we forget."

At every turn we note reminders of the struggle—stones chipped by shells—the scattered débris of recently demolished barricades and the scaffoldings of buildings in reconstruction, for the surrounding quarter, save the buildings immediately adjacent to the center of the defense, was utterly destroyed by incendiary fires. The property loss was enormous; the loss in life among the Europeans, about threescore. It seems incredible that the legations should have withstood for fifty-six days the combined attack of the mobs and of the military forces of the Chinese government whose cannon dominated the entire foreign quarter. It would appear that had the Chinese dared to make a real assault before the defenses were developed, the legations could have

IN THE BRITISH COMPOUND

been taken in a day. But the braggart Boxers were content to bang away from the security of barricaded walls, and to assemble multitudes in the surrounding streets to terrify the foreign devils with their insistent cries of *"Sha, sha!"* "Kill, kill!" If crying could kill Christians, Chinese Christendom would be to-day depopulated — for the melodrama of the siege was played to a demoniac chorus of murderous cries and mutterings from a fanatic populace.

The defenders need no eulogy, their deeds speak for them. Men who were men, and women who were more than men — dared and suffered and fought and lived when it had been far less laborious and far less brave to die.

The defense and relief of the Legations occupied so completely the public mind that little attention was given at the

A LEGATION RESIDENCE

time to the separate siege and ultimate tardy deliverance of
the Pei Tang, the Cathedral and Mission of the French
Catholics. Under the direction of the venerable Bishop of
Peking, Monseigneur Favier, the Catholic flock, to the number of about three thousand, held at bay the hostile population of Peking for two long months; for the siege of the
Pei Tang began before that of the Legations. Moreover,
relief was later in reaching that faithful band of French
Fathers, Sisters of Mercy, and their helpless charges and
converts, the Chinese women and children, who thronged
the spacious buildings of the Catholics' vast enclosure. Fortunately a military guard had been sent to them at the last
moment,—thirty French and ten Italian marines;—and with

THE WORK OF SHOT AND SHELL

the forty rifles thus providentially secured, the Pei Tang
Christians prevailed against an army and a mob. The
church was bombarded continuously for twenty-four consecutive days, during which time more than two thousand shells
and cannon-balls fell within the mission walls. They were
called upon to defend more than fourteen hundred meters of

THE PEI TANG

walls! The enemy used every means, save courage, to
compass their destruction. A forlorn-hope of priests and
wounded marines, led by a bishop, made a sortie, and actually took a cannon from the despicable enemy. Burning
brands were shot over the walls; but the resulting fires were
extinguished by the weary, watchful, famished defenders;

EFFECT OF A MINE EXPLOSION

ONE OF THE SISTERS

breaches made by the Chinese, who were countless, were blocked again by the Christians whose number hourly grew less.

Then mines were laid, and despite the efforts of the defenders to meet them with counter-mines, four of them were successfully completed and exploded with horrible effect.

SITE OF THE ASSASSINATION OF THE GERMAN MINISTER

We never before realized what could be done by the explosion of a subterranean mine; but one glance at the gaping crater near the Cathedral gave us a thrill of horrified amazement and of indignation. We saw a cavity big as a house, marking the spot where one of those artificial volcanoes, made by the cunning Orientals, had vomited death and destruction, annihilating the hospital of the Sisters of Mercy, killing and mangling more than a hundred people, including fifty-three sick native children. Subsequent explosions caused a total of four hundred deaths!

At the Pei Tang, women were in the majority, but, as one of the sisters said, when we expressed surprise at this, "Yes; there were many women; that in itself was an element of strength, it gave more courage to our defenders."

The shattered and defaced Cathedral is, however, being rapidly restored; many of the laborers now shaping the new stones or reshaping the old ones, being the very Boxer fanatics who a year before were battering down its walls. Although it was on Sunday that we visited the Pei Tang, the chisels were playing their industrious staccato round about the house of worship; and ere long the imposing façade will again dominate, with its Christian emblems, the rebellious pagan city whose citizens love not the sight of it.

Peking will not be without conspicuous reminders of the futility of her attempt to cast out the hated alien.

The restored splendor of the Catholic Temple; the great memorial "Pailow," erected in the Ha-Ta Street at the cost of the Chinese government, to mark the site of the

THE NEW GERMAN BARRACKS

assassination of the German Minister; the new railway-stations in the shadow of the Tatar Wall—these structures bear witness to the fact that assaults upon the representatives of the foreigner's religions, governments, and enterprises, can avail nothing: cannot but bring humiliation to the Pekingese. But even more significant to the eyes of the now pacified population of Peking is the new aspect of the legation-quarter, for it has been transformed into an international fortress. Germany has erected spacious barracks for five hundred men in an enclosure that is practically defensible; the United States has provided similar quarters for a hundred and fifty men. Other nations are preparing to garrison Peking with what is virtually an army of defense—under the euphonious title of "Legation Guards."

Western Civilization has profited by the lesson of 1900. Will China profit by the lesson of 1901?

FURTHER READING

Beijing Walks (1992) by Don J. Cohn and Zhang Jingqing contains wonderful scenes from walking tours through this capital city. Stephen Haw's *A Traveller's Guide to China* (1995) covers the same area that Holmes visited in 1901. See also the general survey *China: Its History and Culture* (1995) by W. Scott Horton. Young adults will enjoy Tony Zurlo's *China* (1994).

A lot has been written about the political and economic history of the Far East between 1875 and 1914. For a general overview of the subject, see the following three outstanding college-level textbooks: Kenneth Scott Latourette's *A Short History of the Far East,* Nathaniel Peffer's *The Far East,* and Harold M. Vinacke's History of the *Far East in Modern Times.*

—Dr. Fred L. Israel

CONTRIBUTORS

General Editor FRED L. ISRAEL is an award-winning historian. He received the Scribe's Award from the American Bar Association for his work on the Chelsea House series *The Justices of the United States Supreme Court*. A specialist in American history, he was general editor for Chelsea's *1897 Sears Roebuck Catalog*. Dr. Israel has also worked in association with Arthur M. Schlesinger, jr. on many projects, including *The History of U.S. Presidential Elections* and *The History of U.S. Political Parties*. He is senior consulting editor on the Chelsea House series *Looking into the Past: People, Places, and Customs,* which examines past traditions, customs, and cultures of various nations.

Senior Consulting Editor ARTHUR M. SCHLESINGER, JR. is the preeminent American historian of our time. He won the Pulitzer Prize for his book *The Age of Jackson* (1945), and again for *A Thousand Days* (1965). This chronicle of the Kennedy Administration also won a National Book Award. He has written many other books, including a multi-volume series, *The Age of Roosevelt*. Professor Schlesinger is the Albert Schweitzer Professor of Humanities at the City University of New York, and has been involved in several other Chelsea House projects, including the *American Statesmen* series of biographies on the most prominent figures of early American history.

IRVING WALLACE (1916-1990), whose essay on Burton Holmes is reprinted in the forward to The World 100 Years Ago, is one of the most widely read authors in the world. His books have sold over 200 million copies, and his best-sellers include *The Chapman Report, The Prize, The Man, The Word, The Second Lady,* and *The Miracle*.

INDEX